GOD'S
ABSOLUTES
for
TODAY AND ETERNITY

How to Be Sure
You're Going to Heaven

CLARENCE MAST, M.D.

CREATION
HOUSE

GOD'S ABSOLUTES FOR TODAY AND ETERNITY
by Dr. Clarence Mast
Published by Creation House Books
A Charisma Media Company
600 Rinehart Road
Lake Mary, Florida 32746
www.charismamedia.com

All Scripture quotations are from the Holy Bible, New International Version. Copyright © 1973, 1978, 1984, International Bible Society. Used by permission.

Design Director: Bill Johnson
Cover design by Rachel Lopez

Visit the author's website: www.godsabsolutes.com

Library of Congress Cataloging-in-Publication Data: 2011923397
International Standard Book Number: 978-1-61638-479-1

11 12 13 14 15 — 9 8 7 6 5 4 3 2 1
Printed in Canada

Table *of* Contents

Dedication

This book is dedicated to those who search for a personal relationship with the Lord of lords and King of kings.

Acknowledgments

I AM DEEPLY INDEBTED to the people of Creation House at Charisma Media for taking on the project of my book, including Allen Quain, Ann Stoner, Brenda Davis (also for this book's cover, too), Marilyn Patrick, and Robert Caggiano, as well as to pastors David Twiss and Jason Snyder. Also, my family members, especially my wife Marie, who has been helpful with typing and proofreading and her general support, and my niece, Rosey Dow for her help.

Foreword

WE CAN BE thankful for the incredible books and helps that we have at our disposal in the body of Christ. I am the person I am today in Christ due to, firstly, the Word of God itself. The Bible is our rule of faith and obedience. In addition to this, there have been books and helps that have molded me along with godly people to make me who I am. I have been moved by incredible preaching and shaped by godly teaching through my life. I am glad that I have not been left on my own to grope around in the dark trying to find God.

I am approaching my twenty-fifth anniversary of full-time ministry, and through the years have used many tools in helping people grow in their faith and walk with the Lord. What we are taught in 2 Timothy 3:16–17 is absolutely true: "All Scripture is God-breathed and is useful for teaching, rebuking, correcting and training in righteousness, so that the man of God may be thoroughly equipped for every good work." Through the years, I have used various books and helps that have been a blessing to use to help others understand and digest the scriptures. Many resources have been either too simplistic in their approach at application, or at the other end of the spectrum too in depth for the young believer. This is why I am so excited about Clarence's work that you are about to read. I believe that this work strikes a good balance between the clinical and the practical for the believer through the Word of God. The treatment of basic principles from the Word of God is given proper perspective for the believer of today. Things are not glossed over, but given due diligence in the life of the believer. This is where so many are fearful to tread today. The question "How are we then to live?" comes out clearly in this book. I believe that it will be a blessing to the mature Christian in simply reiterating the truths to which we ascribe in our lives. It will also bless the new believer with a pattern of living the life of faith. In this, Clarence speaks with a clear voice lining up the scriptural standards for living. I thank God for the voice that He has given this servant of His, Clarence, and his willingness to use that voice for God's glory!

I trust that this will be a blessing and encouragement to you as it was for me. May the Lord bless you and allow you to grow in His grace and knowledge through this book.

—REV. DAVID TWISS, LEAD PASTOR
GREEN RIDGE ASSEMBLY OF GOD, SCRANTON,
PENNSYLVANIA

Preface

*H*EAVEN-BOUND? TODAY, MANY people are concerned about where they are going when this life is over. There are many different religions and philosophies out there each espousing what may come after our life on earth is over. There are people who think that if they live a long life of service to humanity, do a lot of good works, and treat other people the way they'd like to be treated, they are going to heaven. There are other people who believe if they go to church three times a week and bring offerings, that they are definitely going to heaven. There are still other people who think that if they say a prayer (even a prayer of salvation) that they are definitely going to heaven. There are other more distorted views that if you kill an infidel (a Christian) you will definitely get some rewards in heaven. Still others think that heaven and hell are here on earth and that humans will become their own God and their destiny is not determined by anyone else. And of course others—agnostics and atheists—believe that we will just evaporate when we die and that's it, no afterlife. It's solely the years we have on this earth, so we can do as we please.

But through the ages, scientists have realized that it's impossible that a human being can come from an amoeba, that there is no upward creation where a simplistic organism can develop into a complex organism, and that there has never been a model for this. And then there's history that centers on the biblical account of Creation from an all-knowing, all-powerful God we can't understand or comprehend; where all power and wisdom come from.

There has been documentation before and after the birth, life, death, and resurrection of Jesus Christ in history. With our Judeo-Christian heritage through the Bible, Jesus shows us (as churchgoing Americans, for example) that there are some guidelines you can use to determine whether you are going to heaven or not. The guidelines are very specific with no gray areas. They are absolutely absolute—yet they are very simple.

I hope you will find this book edifying, but most important, if you're not ready for the Rapture or Judgment Day, both of which are close, today is the day to get ready. Today is the day to know for sure.

That is what this book is all about. If you are not redeemed, I pray you will experience God's glory, His redemptive power, and an infusion of the Person of the Holy Spirit into your life so you will be ready. There is no church membership of any kind, nor any position in the church, that could guarantee you entrance to the kingdom of God.

Introduction

*I*HAVE BEEN A primary care physician for thirty-seven years. Through these years I've had many opportunities to observe and assess human behavior. As a Christian, I've also had the opportunity to interact and intercede for my patients. I realized that no matter how destitute or desperate my patients might be, there but for the grace of God go I—nobody is hopeless with God's redemption, salvation, and healing.

I can also say with the apostle Paul that I'm "the chief of sinners," as he said he was. My rejection of God early in my life certainly fits in that category as well as other failures.

One of the driving forces for this book was an evening at church during which our deacons and their wives were being introduced and they were to give their testimonies. One of the deacon's wives indicated that she had gone forward during an invitation time at her church and prayed the Sinner's Prayer, but the next night she did it again and, I presume, the third night she did it again until finally the church leaders told her that once she had prayed the prayer of salvation she didn't need to come back. Once she prayed and believed, she was saved. Sadly, that is not the complete truth. For God has made it very clear in the Bible in Romans 8 that when we experience salvation we will also experience the presence of the Holy Spirit in our lives. We will experience the joy of salvation and His blessed hope.

A short time after that evening at church, in a discussion with our pastor, he indicated that possibly as many as 50

1

percent of the church members didn't know the Lord. It is for this reason that I wrote this book to the Christian church. If you've gone to church for one year, ten years, or fifty years; if you've never been aware of the Holy Spirit in your life with His redemptive power and the joy of His salvation; if you have not turned away from your old sinful ways and have not been desiring to serve the Lord with all your heart and all your mind and all your soul; then you'll certainly need to ask the God of this universe where you stand in your relationship with Him. You certainly can ask Him whether you're going to heaven or not. You can ask if there is anything in your life that you are doing that is displeasing Him. You can ask Him if there is any unforgiveness in your heart that you need to surrender at the foot of his cross.

God's laws are absolute. His love is unending, but his judgment is sure. The Bible says we're to work out our salvation with fear and trembling. Salvation is free. We can't buy it with a price, but once we're redeemed He expects us to guard it like a precious jewel.

Where is your heart today? What are the innermost desires of your heart and spirit? Is it to love the Lord with all your heart, mind, and soul? Or is it to serve yourself with pleasure? The Bible says that no one can serve two masters. You can't love the Lord with all your heart on Sunday and live like the world and serve your own desires Monday through Saturday. God has a very marked displeasure for people who are trying to serve two masters.

It has been my observation after many years in primary care medicine that people who try to serve two masters will usually destroy themselves physically, emotionally, financially, and otherwise.

God's calling and election are sure. As you read this book,

determine in your mind to serve Him with all your heart and to receive nothing from Satan or his gang.

May the presence of God's Holy Spirit minister to you as you read this book. God bless you.

—CLARENCE MAST, MD

1

Love

*T*HE FIRST COMMANDMENT is that we're to love the Lord our God with all our heart, mind, and soul. One of the most important things that we can do as Christians is affirm our love for God the Father, God the son Jesus, and God the Holy Spirit every day, just as we would affirm a family relationship here on this earth. We need to affirm our love to God so much more. God created us to worship Him, to love Him, to adore Him, and to honor Him willingly. He could have created beings that would have the innate nature to constantly worship Him like angels do. He could have created humans with that same frame of mind. But He wanted us to serve Him of our own volition with all our hearts and to the best of our ability. So, it's imperative that before we receive anything from God, we let Him know that we love Him with all our heart, all our mind, all our soul, and with our total being.

> Jesus replied: "'Love the Lord your God with all your heart and with all your soul and with all your mind.' This is the first and greatest commandment. And the second is like it: 'Love your neighbor as yourself.' All the Law and the Prophets hang on these two commandments."
>
> —MATTHEW 22:37, 38

If you don't believe there is a God, the God of Abraham, Isaac, and Jacob, ask Him if He is the God of the Bible. If He is who He claims He is, ask Him to show you in a definite way. The Bible says if we ask God we'll receive an answer from Him. If we really desire in our hearts to know the true living God, He will show us.

> For God so loved the world that he gave his one and only Son, that whoever believes in him shall not perish but have eternal life.
>
> —JOHN 3:16

Our God is full of love and compassion with tremendous mercy. The Bible says that it's His desire that none of us should perish, not even one. God's love is so great that He can forgive even the most vile offender. It is hard to conceptualize a God with so much love and compassion for His children that He gave His only begotten Son Jesus for our sins, for our redemption, for our salvation, and for our healing. He even promises to provide our needs according to His riches in glory.

God's laws are eternal. They are permanent. They always apply to every situation. He honors His children who obey His laws. Fortunately, God always looks on our hearts and sees the desires of our hearts and not our external expressions.

What is the desire on your heart? Do you get up every morning and say, "Lord, I desire You more than anything else. I want to honor You in everything I do today. I praise You for your goodness and mercy. I love You for redeeming me and saving my soul; for creating me; for protecting me; and for caring for me"?

You will seek me and find me when you seek me with all your heart. I will be found by you," declares the LORD.

—JEREMIAH 29:13

That everyone who believes may have eternal life in him." For God so loved the world that he gave his one and only Son, that whoever believes in him shall not perish but have eternal life. For God did not send his Son into the world to condemn the world, but to save the world through him. Whoever believes in him is not condemned, but whoever does not believe stands condemned already because they have not believed in the name of God's one and only Son.

—JOHN 3:15–18

You, God, are my God, earnestly I seek you; I thirst for you, my whole being longs for you, in a dry and parched land where there is no water. I have seen you in the sanctuary and beheld your power and your glory. Because your love is better than life, my lips will glorify you. I will praise you as long as I live, and in your name I will lift up my hands. I will be fully satisfied as with the richest of foods; with singing lips my mouth will praise you.

—PSALM 63:1–5

Praise the LORD, my soul; all my inmost being, praise his holy name. Praise the LORD, my soul, and forget not all his benefits—who forgives all your sins and heals all your diseases, who redeems your life from the pit and crowns you with love and compassion, who satisfies your desires with good things so that your youth is renewed like the eagle's.

—PSALM 103:1–5

Praise the LORD, all you nations; extol him, all you peoples. For great is his love toward us, and the faithfulness of the LORD endures forever. Praise the LORD.

—PSALM 117

2

Forgive *and* Be Forgiven

*I*N THE LORD's Prayer Jesus specifically says, "Forgive us our trespasses, as we forgive those who trespass against us." Forgiveness needs to be on our minds constantly. As Christians we are tested every day. We are tested by the world. We might be tested by fellow Christians and fellow churchgoers. But forgiveness is not an option. To come into the presence of the Lord with thanksgiving we need to forgive all those who have offended us in any way. That might encompass members of our families, members of our community, members of our church, our coworkers, and or our boss. It might include those who deride us because of our Christian faith or those who slander us. Total forgiveness leads to joy and peace. There is nothing as liberating as forgiveness.

You can see this in the joy and peace of Corrie ten Boom. In her book, *the Hiding Place*, she describes the Lord's protection because of bed lice that kept the soldiers from molesting them. Many years later, Corrie ten Boom met one of the officers who had tortured her and she expressed to him her total forgiveness.

Nothing is as liberating for the Christian as constant alertness for the need to forgive. Sometimes we're not actually deeply offended or hurt, but we might be disturbed by little things in the way people treat us. This could be a family member. Even if they don't treat us with respect or honor, forgive them every time there is any kind of offense. Jesus' total forgiveness for our sins has a tremendous liberating effect. The same is true as we forgive others who might offend us in even minor ways.

If we know of the offense, we need to be active in the forgiveness. Forgiveness is supernatural. Jesus shed His blood for our forgiveness. It is natural to hold grudges on the human side of things, but on the Jesus side of things, forgiveness is everything.

> Then Peter came to Jesus and asked, "Lord, how many times shall I forgive my brother or sister who sins against me? Up to seven times?" Jesus answered, "I tell you, not seven times, but seventy-seven times."
> —MATTHEW 18:21, 22

Notice the importance of forgiveness with Jesus' instructions in the scriptures. He says that if we are praying and we know we have an offense with someone else in that place, then before we start our petitions with the Lord, we must go and settle things with the person with whom we have the offense.

When someone prays the Sinner's Prayer to receive salvation, if they aren't aware of any hatred or hostility or unforgiveness they have toward another person, I think the Lord extends His total forgiveness freely. However, if they have a grudge against someone, God makes it very clear in the scriptures that unless we forgive them first, He won't forgive us. Many times when people go forward for salvation, if they don't receive the cleansing miracle of God's deliverance at that time the first place they need to look in their life is unforgiveness. In Mark 11:25, 26, the Word of God absolutely says that if we stand praying, forgive so that God will forgive our trespasses and further, if we do not forgive, neither will our Father in heaven forgive us. And if they aren't aware that there's someone with whom they have a problem with unforgiveness, they need to ask the Lord to show them if that is a problem or if there is any other issue that is interfering with their redemption.

> And forgive us our debts, as we also have forgiven our debtors.
> —MATTHEW 6:12

> Therefore, if you are offering your gift at the altar and there remember that your brother or sister has something against you, leave your gift there in front of the altar. First go and be reconciled to them; then come and offer your gift.
> —MATTHEW 5:23, 24

God is always pleased when our desire is to please Him with all our body, mind, and soul. If we ask the Lord if there is anything in our life that is displeasing to Him—unforgiveness or anything else—He will show it to us so we can take care of it. And if God does show you what you need to do, even if it requires communicating with another person, do it.

I have found that the sooner I do it, the easier it is and God's grace is always sufficient. His renewal is always there for us, and His peace and joy are more valuable than the benefit of any grudge we might hold through our personal ego.

> Search me, God, and know my heart; test me and know my anxious thoughts. See if there is any offensive way in me, and lead me in the way everlasting.
> —PSALM 139:23, 24

As the Father has loved me, so have I loved you. Now remain in my love. If you keep my commands, you will remain in my love, just as I have kept my Father's commands and remain in his love. I have told you this so that my joy may be in you and that your joy may be complete. My command is this: Love each other as I have loved you. Greater love has no one than this: to lay down one's life for one's friends.

—John 15:9–13

3

Repent

*T*HE BIBLE TELLS us to repent with fear and trembling, to guard our hearts, and place high value on our salvation. God said that if we turn away from our wicked ways and seek Him with all our heart, He will make us a new creation. The Bible makes it very clear that when someone becomes a Christian, something will happen in their life. Instead of seeking after the world with all its desires, we'll seek after the Lord in all His majesty and honor, glory, power, omniscience, and wisdom. Jesus said He's not about the king of this world, but about the kingdom of God and bringing it to this world.

> Repent, then, and turn to God, so that your sins may be wiped out, that times of refreshing may come from the Lord, and that he may send the Messiah, who has been appointed for you—even Jesus.
> —ACTS 3:19, 20

Some people immediately experience the transformation. For other people, the transformation is a journey. The Bible says that if we repent and turn to the Lord and totally commit to the Lord, there are benefits: love, joy, peace, patience, kindness, goodness, faithfulness, gentleness, and self-control. There is no price on the peace that Jesus gives us or the joy He puts into our souls. A lot of people are searching for happiness, but the joy of salvation only comes from the King of kings and the Prince of Peace.

> Therefore, if anyone is in Christ, the new creation has come: The old has gone, the new is here!
> —2 CORINTHIANS 5:7

When we interact with our holy God and we repent, something happens. If you keep on doing the same old things you've always done and nothing happens, then you need to start asking God why. When we repent, the Bible says, we'll turn from our wicked ways. We'll become a new creation. People will notice that we are different, and the first change will be from the heart. The external changes might not show up for a while. So, let's be slow to condemn someone who has repented and desires to serve the Lord, but still has external issues such as smoking or drinking. One thing is sure—as we seek the Lord and honor Him with our whole being, He'll give us deliverance from addictions and desires our human nature conjures up.

> But the fruit of the Spirit is love, joy, peace, forbearance, kindness, goodness, faithfulness, gentleness and self-control. Against such things there is no law.
> —GALATIANS 5:22, 23

> In those days John the Baptist came, preaching in the wilderness of Judea and saying, "Repent, for the kingdom of heaven has come near."

> From that time on Jesus began to preach, "Repent, for the kingdom of heaven has come near."
> —MATTHEW 3:1–2; 4:17

They went out and preached that people should repent.

—MARK 6:12

Peter replied, "Repent and be baptized, every one of you, in the name of Jesus Christ for the forgiveness of your sins. And you will receive the gift of the Holy Spirit. The promise is for you and your children and for all who are far off—for all whom the Lord our God will call."

—ACTS 2:38–39

4

Be Filled

THE BIBLE SAYS that we are to be filled with the Holy Spirit as a result of our salvation. It is interesting that in the great salvation book, Romans, in chapter 8, Paul describes how we will know if we are a Christian or not. That comes before the great salvation chapter 10. Paul says in Romans 8:1, "Therefore, there is now no condemnation for those who are in Christ Jesus." Romans 8:2 says, "Because through Christ Jesus the law of the Spirit of life set me free from the law of sin and death."

He continues:

> In order that the righteous requirements of the law might be fully met in us, who do not live according to the sinful nature but according to the Spirit. Those who live according to the sinful nature have their minds set on what that nature desires; but those who live in accordance with the Spirit have their minds set on what the Spirit desires. The mind of sinful man is death, but the mind controlled by the Spirit is life and peace; the sinful mind is hostile to God. It does not submit to God's law, nor can it do so. Those controlled by the sinful nature cannot please God.
>
> —ROMANS 8:4–8

So it's very clear that God is outlining how we can determine whether we are serving God or not. He very distinctly says that to be carnally minded is death but to be spiritually minded is life and peace, indicating that our innermost desires are everything to God, not that we might not fail or be imperfect, but if the desire on our heart is to serve him with all we have, God honors that tremendously.

He goes on to say:

> You, however, are controlled not by the sinful nature but by the Spirit, if the Spirit of God lives in you. And if anyone does not have the Spirit of Christ, he does not belong to Christ. So these verses show how important it's to know that you have the spirit of the Most high God dwelling in you.
>
> —ROMANS 8:9

He goes on:

> But if Christ is in you, your body is dead because of sin, yet your spirit is alive because of righteousness.
>
> —ROMANS 8:10

So, God's spirit is His righteousness for us.

> And if the Spirit of him who raised Jesus from the dead is living in you, he who raised Christ from the dead will also give life to your mortal bodies through his Spirit, who lives in you.
>
> —ROMANS 8:11

God's Holy Spirit is the One who will quicken us at the Rapture. Are you ready? Do you know that you have the Holy Spirit? If not, let's make sure.

For if you live according to the sinful nature, you
will die; but if by the Spirit you put to death the mis-
deeds of the body, you will live.

—Romans 8:13

Again, if you are living to please your own desires of your
flesh and that's in your heart, you've got a problem.

Because those who are led by the Spirit of God are
sons of God. For you did not receive a spirit that
makes you a slave again to fear, but you received the
Spirit of sonship. And by him we cry, "Abba, Father."
The Spirit himself testifies with our spirit that we
are God's children. Now if we are children, then we
are heirs—heirs of God and co-heirs with Christ, if
indeed we share in his sufferings in order that we
may also share in his glory.

—Romans 8:14–17

These verses indicate that the presence of the Holy Spirit
for a Christian is absolutely necessary. In my own case, the
presence of the Holy Spirit at salvation and at baptism was
overwhelming. I realize that might not be the case for every
person. For some people the period of repentance could be
over a period of months until they come to the Lord and see
God change their hearts.

One thing I've noticed in praying one-on-one with a prayer
partner, and some of the prayer partners I've prayed with in
the past, as soon as we start praying, the presence of the Holy
Spirit is immediate. You're very much aware of the presence
of the Holy Spirit. I'd encourage you, if you're not sure about
the presence of the Holy Spirit in your life, why not ask God?
Ask God if you are going to heaven. Ask God to give you the
assurance of salvation by giving you discernment about the

presence of the Holy Spirit in your life. Ask Him specifically if there is any unforgiveness in your life. Ask Him to give you a prayer partner who knows you and is filled with His Holy Spirit, so that when you start to pray and ask for the presence of the Holy Spirit, He will come and meet with you and be present with you while your entreaty is being made to the holy of holies.

The Lord is gentle. Some Christians might know the Lord and yet have never been aware of the present of the Holy Spirit in their lives. I find this to be unusual, however, as God's Spirit absolutely permeates our beings as we sell out to Him.

> But you will receive power when the Holy Spirit comes on you; and you will be my witnesses in Jerusalem, and in all Judea and Samaria, and to the ends of the earth."
>
> —Acts 1:8

> Peter replied, "Repent and be baptized, every one of you, in the name of Jesus Christ for the forgiveness of your sins. And you will receive the gift of the Holy Spirit. The promise is for you and your children and for all who are far off—for all whom the Lord our God will call."
>
> —Acts 2:38, 39

> After they prayed, the place where they were meeting was shaken. And they were all filled with the Holy Spirit and spoke the word of God boldly.
>
> —Acts 4:31

5

Ask *and* You Shall Receive

HROUGHOUT THE BIBLE, the Lord encourages us to ask about anything we need. He said to ask with faith, believing as we speak, that we will have it. He says that if we have faith the size of a mustard seed we can move mountains. (See Matthew 17:20.) Nothing is impossible with God. It's the Lord's desire, as you'll notice in the Lord's Prayer, to have His kingdom and His power to come to this earth through the power of the Holy Spirit and through the redemption of Jesus. He says that we have not because we asked not.

> If any of you lacks wisdom, you should ask God, who gives generously to all without finding fault, and it will be given to you. But when you ask, you must believe and not doubt, because the one who doubts is like a wave of the sea, blown and tossed by the wind.
>
> —JAMES 1:5–6

> He replied, "Because you have so little faith. Truly I tell you, if you have faith as small as a mustard seed, you can say to this mountain, 'Move from here to there, and it will move. Nothing will be impossible for you."
>
> —MATTHEW 17:20

For with God nothing will be impossible."

—LUKE 1:37, NKJV

As I think of the things that have happened in my life, one of my biggest mistakes has been when I haven't asked Him first about everything and even little things. But obviously we should ask Him about every major decision, like which school to go to, who to marry, which investments to make, what to do with my life, what profession to go into. The Lord says to seek His face with all our heart, all our mind, all our soul, and He also says there's much greater power when two people pray together than one, in which case a prayer partner can become valuable as we ask and seek the Lord.

> You desire but do not have, so you kill. You covet but you cannot get what you want, so you quarrel and fight. You do not have because you do not ask God.
>
> —JAMES 4:2

> Hear my voice when I call, LORD; be merciful to me and answer me. My heart says of you, "Seek his face!" Your face, LORD, I will seek.
>
> —PSALM 27:7–8

The Bible says we are supposed to pray without ceasing. You know, we can pray as we're driving. We can pray as we're eating. We can pray as we're working on many occasions. We can pray that God will give us wisdom for every task. We can pray for healing for ourselves, for our family, and for our friends. We can pray for those who need salvation. We can pray for God's blessing and goodness in financial areas. The Bible tells us to prosper, even as our soul prospers, so the first challenge to prosperity for us as Christians is to make sure our soul is prospering.

Pray continually.

—1 Thessalonians 5:17

Dear friend, I pray that you may enjoy good health and that all may go well with you, even as your soul is getting along well.

—3 John 1:2

If you believe, you will receive whatever you ask for in prayer.

—Matthew 21:22

6

No Condemnation

ONE OF THE first things a Christian needs to notice in his or her life is that there is no condemnation for those who are in Christ Jesus. If the Lord has truly redeemed you, instead of condemning those who might have done something to you on a personal level that you don't agree with or you don't believe is right, pray for them with the love of Jesus. The power of God will come upon them and redeem them from sin and death. When I look at public figures—who could be in ministry, government, or politics—on a personal level, there cannot be any condemnation because they are a child of the King of kings just as I am, and there but for the grace of God could be me. Remember, if you are a condemning person who claims to be a Christian, you need to ask God if you're going to heaven or not. And if we confess and repent of that spirit, He will deliver us.

> For God did not send his Son into the world to condemn the world, but to save the world through him.
> —JOHN 3:17

> Therefore, there is now no condemnation for those who are in Christ Jesus,
> —ROMANS 8:1

> But I tell you, love your enemies and pray for those
> who persecute you.
>
> —MATTHEW 5:44

Many Christians get confused. For example, people in politics are sworn to uphold the Constitution of our country. Our country was founded on Christian principles. If they break the Constitution, we, the people who have all the constitutional rights of this nation, need to stand up for the Constitution or otherwise we'll lose those rights. But be mindful. Our leaders represent our nation. A poll taken about fifteen years ago by the *Wall Street Journal* reported that a significant majority of Americans lie regularly—but when a very similar poll was taken again, that majority had *increased*, instead of declining. Obviously, our democracy and our nation will not survive where there is no truth or where no one keeps his word, where everybody is full of greed and cheating.

Our world has changed drastically in the last fifty years. When I was a child, my father bought a farm on a handshake. There was no contracts. There was his word and the banker's word, and that was all they needed. Then, even our non-Christian neighbors for the most part kept their word. If they told you they were going to do something, you could take it to the bank. They honored Judeo-Christian principles.

As Christians, we need to attempt in every part of our life to have absolute integrity to the best of our ability. Realizing that while no one is perfect, we need to make every effort to do that.

> When Abram was ninety-nine years old, the LORD
> appeared to him and said, "I am God Almighty;
> walk before me faithfully and be blameless.
>
> —GENESIS 17:1

Be perfect, therefore, as your heavenly Father is perfect.

—MATTHEW 5:48

Let perseverance finish its work so that you may be mature and complete, not lacking anything.

—JAMES 1:4

BE MERCIFUL

Jesus told us to love our enemies, pray for them who spitefully use you, and to be gentle. Remember, a soft answer turns away wrath. If you're criticized and you respond with hatred and hostility, then you need to examine your own heart. The Bible says that if you do that, your actions are not from Jesus and not from the Holy Spirit. So we need to be very aware of how we respond to people who might falsely accuse us.

Normally, if we're guilty, we'll respond with hostility. If we're not guilty, we can defend ourselves, but we can respond with love and not with hatred. Again, some Christians get confused on the right of our country to defend its integrity, our borders, and our Constitution. While we love our personal enemies, God makes it very clear in the Old Testament that we do have the privilege and ability to defend our country and our Constitution.

God is pretty dramatic in how He handled the enemies of Israel, when Israel was serving Him. There were not many occasions when God told Israel to "Treat them gently. Talk them out of terrorizing us, and we'll see if we can't change their minds." Rather, He was very swift and direct. The enemy would be very aware that the hand of God was working for His people who loved Him in the Old Testament.

Let everyone be subject to the governing authorities, for there is no authority except that which God has established. The authorities that exist have been established by God. Consequently, whoever rebels against the authority is rebelling against what God has instituted, and those who do so will bring judgment on themselves. For rulers hold no terror for those who do right, but for those who do wrong. Do you want to be free from fear of the one in authority? Then do what is right and you will be commended. For the one in authority is God's servant for your good. But if you do wrong, be afraid, for rulers do not bear the sword for no reason. They are God's servants, agents of wrath to bring punishment on the wrongdoer. Therefore, it is necessary to submit to the authorities, not only because of possible punishment but also as a matter of conscience. This is also why you pay taxes, for the authorities are God's servants, who give their full time to governing. Give to everyone what you owe them: If you owe taxes, pay taxes; if revenue, then revenue; if respect, then respect; if honor, then honor.

—ROMANS 13:1–7

GIVE WITH JOY

The Bible indicates that we need to give to the Lord generously, and with a joyful heart. A lot of Christians feel like they need to give 10 percent of their income to the Lord. I think that's a good place to start. However, I think it's still important to give where the Lord leads you to give. You'll hear a lot of pastors say, "Give your money to your local church." If your local church is full of the power of the Holy Spirit, serving the Lord, bringing people to the Lord, and the Lord tells you to give, by all means give. But, ask Him exactly where your money should go instead of blindly doing it. We're going to be accountable in heaven. We need to give out of generosity, and we also need to ask where and to whom we're supposed to give. We're giving it to organizations that are winning the lost for His kingdom. If you attend a church that does not sow into God's kingdom, change it if you can, otherwise get out and attend another church that honors Him.

Each of you should give what you have decided in your heart to give, not reluctantly or under compulsion, for God loves a cheerful giver.

—2 CORINTHIANS 9:7

God also says that we need to give, believing He'll supply all our needs according to His riches in glory. (See Philippians 4:19.) In response, we'll be blessed in a manner that is shaken, pressed down, and running over. He'll meet all our needs. He says, as we believe in our heart with faith like the grain of a mustard seed, He'll give us the desires of our heart. I believe we're going to have to exercise this a lot in the coming days as things get tougher financially. In my own experience, when you have your greatest need, start to give, and if you can only give a small amount, you need to give and believe that God will meet your needs. He always meets our needs according to Malachi 3:10,11, which says that as we give, God will open up the windows of heaven and pour out a blessing that we can not hold and further more He will rebuke Satan the devourer for our sakes.

And my God will meet all your needs according to the riches of his glory in Christ Jesus.

—PHILIPPIANS 4:19

We need to set goals with our giving. In my own experience, after God had called me into a ministry of giving to donate a certain amount in my lifetime, and as He blessed me so I could meet that goal, I started believing Him to give more in my lifetime. If I meet the second goal, even at my age, I'm going to have a new goal. I'm expecting and believing to meet that second goal, in my lifetime if the Lord tarries.

Jesus sat down opposite the place where the offerings were put and watched the crowd putting their money into the temple treasury. Many rich people threw in large amounts. But a poor widow came and put in two very small copper coins, worth only a few cents. Calling his disciples to him, Jesus said, "Truly I tell you, this poor widow has put more into the treasury than all the others. They all gave out of their wealth; but she, out of her poverty, put in everything—all she had to live on."

—MARK 12:41–44

7

Bless *the* Lord

*B*LESS THE LORD, all my soul, and all that is within me. The Bible encourages us to worship the Lord and praise Him for everything. Praise God in all things. Even when things are going bad, we're supposed to bless the Lord and praise Him. Singing God's praises for His majesty and His glory really destroys the power of Satan. The glory of God is so powerful, so redeeming, and so strong. Who can stand against Him?

> I will exalt you, my God the King; I will praise your name for ever and ever. Every day I will praise you and extol your name for ever and ever. Great is the LORD and most worthy of praise; his greatness no one can fathom.
>
> —PSALM 145:1–3

Just as the Bible says we're to praise the Lord in all things, the Lord tells us to bless them that curse you. That could be tough. That is, we pray for the redemption of those who might curse us or hate us and ask God to bless them with total redemption. He'll take care of us, and if they refuse to be redeemed, God says vengeance is His. We don't have to exercise it. He says He'll repay and that we don't have to fret about it. He also says that those who slander the righteous are an abomination to Him. So God has a checking account, and He doesn't forget. But He is longsuffering with us, and even longsuffering with our enemies and those who curse Him.

> Praise the LORD, my soul; all my inmost being, praise his holy name. Praise the LORD, my soul, and forget not all his benefits.
>
> —PSALM 103:1–2

> Praise the LORD. Praise God in his sanctuary; praise him in his mighty heavens. Praise him for his acts of power; praise him for his surpassing greatness. Praise him with the sounding of the trumpet, praise him with the harp and lyre, praise him with timbrel and dancing, praise him with the strings and pipe, praise him with the clash of cymbals, praise him with resounding cymbals. Let everything that has breath praise the LORD. Praise the LORD.
>
> —PSALM 150

Again, this is on a personal level. We can certainly pray for the terrorists to be delivered from the power of Satan. But, we also have the right and duty to defend our Constitution. I believe we need to continue to defend our country and protect our borders as necessary, since God gives our government the right to defend itself from being annihilated by an enemy just as could have happened in World War II if we had not defended ourselves.

Remember, we bless the Lord when we serve our creator with the deepest desires of our heart and honor His commandments and His Word. We also bless Him with our tithes and offerings because of our covenant relationship with Him. Because we have access to the Kingdom of God through Jesus Christ, we need to continue the verbal blessings in the Abrahamic tradition to our children and grandchildren. Children that are blessed in the Lord's name with favor, wisdom, protection, provision, and with a desire to serve the living God, thrive much better than those who are not.

Do not take revenge, my dear friends, but leave room for God's wrath, for it is written: "It is mine to avenge; I will repay," says the Lord.

—ROMANS 12:19

8

No Other Gods

*P*AUL NOTED IN his travels that some of the people of his day were serving many, many gods. They had temples to many gods, even to the unknown God. But we have specific instructions. God makes it exquisitely clear we are to serve the God of Abraham, Isaac, Jacob, and Him only are we to serve. Historians have documented the life of Jesus, even historians who hated Him. Jesus is the only "prophet" who ever rose from the dead. No other religions claimed to have prophets who rose from the dead. Much of our history is based on the death, burial, and resurrection of Jesus Christ.

How do we know that Jesus is true? Again, we go back to being filled with the Holy Spirit, since by His presence, we know that we are the children of the King of kings. He says that whenever two or three of us are gathered together, the Holy Spirit's presence will be there with us. Just ask Him. He is the Holy Spirit. He is gentle. The Person of the Holy Spirit is very gentle. Ask for His presence and be assured that Jesus is God, and that the person of the Holy Spirit is God with us.

You shall have no other gods before me.
—EXODUS 20:3

Paul then stood up in the meeting of the Areopagus and said: "People of Athens! I see that in every way you are very religious. For as I walked around and looked carefully at your objects of worship, I even found an altar with this inscription: TO AN UNKNOWN GOD. So you are ignorant of the very thing you worship—and this is what I am going to proclaim to you.

—Acts 17:22–23

For those who are led by the Spirit of God are the children of God. The Spirit you received does not make you slaves, so that you live in fear again; rather, the Spirit you received brought about your adoption to sonship. And by him we cry, "Abba, Father." The Spirit himself testifies with our spirit that we are God's children. Now if we are children, then we are heirs—heirs of God and co-heirs with Christ, if indeed we share in his sufferings in order that we may also share in his glory.

—Romans 8:14–17

For where two or three gather in my name, there am I with them."

—Matthew 18:20

So you also must be ready, because the Son of Man will come at an hour when you do not expect him.

—Matthew 24:44

Therefore, my dear friends, as you have always obeyed—not only in my presence, but now much more in my absence—continue to work out your salvation with fear and trembling.

—Philippians 2:12

For it is by grace you have been saved, through faith—and this is not from yourselves, it is the gift of God—not by works, so that no one can boast.

—Ephesians 2:8–9

Expect His Return

The Bible tells us to live every day in such a way as we expect the return of Jesus. It also encourages us to work our salvation with great fear and trembling. Obviously, salvation is by the grace of God. We can't pay for it. Jesus already paid the price for it. But the gist of this message, to me, is that we can't pray the prayer of salvation, repent, and become a child of the King of kings, but continue to live like the world. If we continue to live like the world, no matter what's happened, we might be surprised on the day we meet the Lord.

"Not everyone who says to me, 'Lord, Lord,' will enter the kingdom of heaven, but only the one who does the will of my Father who is in heaven. Many will say to me on that day, 'Lord, Lord, did we not prophesy in your name and in your name drive out demons and in your name perform many miracles?' Then I will tell them plainly, 'I never knew you. Away from me, you evildoers!'"

—Matthew 7:21–23

"Why do you call me, 'Lord, Lord,' and do not do what I say?"

—Luke 6:46

Jesus says that many churchgoing people have done great miracles in His name, even casting out demons, and Jesus will tell them to depart into everlasting darkness, "I never knew you." The saddest thing for churchgoing America today is that non-Christians who reject God are on the way to a God-less eternity. They know where they're going. They expect damnation. If you ask them, they'll invariably expect to go down to wherever hell is, but they say they're going. They won't be surprised. But the biggest surprises could be for the people who are going to church, who are not living for Him, who don't have the power of the Holy Spirit in their lives, and continue doing whatever they please after having said a prayer at some point in time. Jesus is going to say "I never knew you. I don't know you. If you truly knew Me, you wouldn't be lying about things. You wouldn't be unrepentant if you sinned. You wouldn't live a life of damnation" (author's paraphrase).

That's why it behooves us to constantly ask the Lord if there is anything in our lives that is displeasing to Him. Every day, ask Him. There's no person you need to please more than God the Father, God the Son Jesus, and God the Holy Spirit. If you're displeasing Him, He'll let you know. Stop doing whatever He shows you is wrong between you and Him. Repent, and turn to the Lord.

> Restore to me the joy of your salvation and grant me
> a willing spirit, to sustain me.
> —Psalm 51:12

I believe in the assurance of salvation. I believe God gives us time to repent, but I also believe that our hardened hearts and turning away from God after saying a prayer countless years ago will not save us. When you pray the prayer of salvation, something has to happen. The joy of His salvation needs to be present. It needs to be a total realization that God has redeemed you from your sin. You may also experience sorrow for the pain and suffering you caused Jesus on the cross, because He had to bear our sins on the cross. Some of us have had massive failures in our lives. But a repentant soul who loves the Lord with all His heart brings great joy to the angels in heaven. Choose this day who you will serve. Is it God? Or is it Satan? Determine in your heart to serve the Lord with all you are. Come into His gates with thanksgiving and praise. Forgive every day anybody who has hurt you. Forgive. Forgive especially when you go to church. If you have a fight with your spouse that morning, make sure you forgive, because if you don't forgive, that automatically breaks your entrance into the holy of holies. The Bible says if we confess our sins, He is faithful and just to forgive us and cleanse us from all unrighteousness. He says that we are to seek the kingdom of God and all His righteousness and all these things will be added to us.

We serve a mighty God. His majesty, His power, His glory, and His kingdom are unmatched.

> I tell you that in the same way there will be more rejoicing in heaven over one sinner who repents than over ninety-nine righteous persons who do not need to repent.
>
> —LUKE 15:7

> But if serving the LORD seems undesirable to you, then choose for yourselves this day whom you will serve, whether the gods your ancestors served beyond the Euphrates, or the gods of the Amorites, in whose land you are living. But as for me and my household, we will serve the LORD."
>
> —JOSHUA 24:15

If we confess our sins, he is faithful and just and will forgive us our sins and purify us from all unrighteousness.

—1 JOHN 1:9

But seek first his kingdom and his righteousness, and all these things will be given to you as well.

—MATTHEW 6:33

9

The Lord's Prayer

*I*F YOU WANT to get an appreciation for what God desires for our heart, for our nation, for us as Christian people, all we have to do is look at His prayer. The first part of the prayer is, "Our father which art in heaven." Jesus acknowledges that His Father God is in heaven. When Jesus left this earth, God the Holy Spirit came to dwell with us at Pentecost.

> This, then, is how you should pray: "Our Father in heaven, hallowed be your name, your kingdom come, your will be done, on earth as it is in heaven. Give us today our daily bread. And forgive us our debts, as we also have forgiven our debtors. And lead us not into temptation, but deliver us from the evil one."
>
> —MATTHEW 6:9–13

He said, "Hallowed be thy name." In essence, He is saying, "I know You, I worship You, I praise You, I bless Your holy name," and that we should pray this prayer honoring our Creator, our Redeemer, and our Provider.

Then He says, "Thy kingdom come" and He indicates that the kingdom is coming from heaven with God's power, glory, majesty, redemption, salvation, wisdom, love, protection, provision, and favor. Everything that's entailed by the kingdom is to come down to this earth, so the glory of God can be manifested in His children. And as you worship and praise Him, enter into His glory and you will see the tremendous power of the glory of God.

"Thy will be done, on this earth as it is in heaven," tells us what God's will is for us as His church. God's will is our total redemption, total forgiveness, total healing, and total provision. His will is that we'll be a people who honor Him in every way. He'll give us grace for every situation. His will is that we will partake of His favor and wisdom on a daily basis.

Then He says, "Give us this day our daily bread." We've not experienced a famine in this country since the Great Depression. In my understanding, there were three years of drought during that time. We need to be thankful that God provides food for us and provides for our physical needs on a daily basis as well. As we embark on possibly our next Great Depression, and if we have three years of drought again, people in our nation will be starving. Our people have become a people who reject God, with a leader who proclaims we are no longer a Christian nation. But God assures us that He'll heal us, He'll give us leaders who honor Him if the Christians in our nation will repent. (See 2 Chronicles 7:14.) I personally believe that if Christians of this nation would repent and turn to the Lord, even if it's a small proportion of them of maybe fewer than 50 percent of this nation, our nation would begin turning around. But a nation that does not honor God He will judge, and His judgment will bring desolation and poverty, disease, and loss of freedom.

If you look at many nations around the world whose people have turned their backs on the Lord, for the most part the masses of people are in poverty. There are still many rich people, but the masses of people are in poverty. There is essentially no middle class in many of these nations. More and more, we're becoming a nation of elitists with the very rich and soon-to-be very poor. The middle class in our nation is disappearing.

Next He says, "Forgive us our trespasses as we forgive those who trespass against us." As we've noted, the importance of forgiveness is that God will not forgive us unless we forgive others, and it is so critically important.

Then He says, "Lead us not into temptation but deliver us from evil." I think this passage in the Lord's Prayer is a key part that makes this prayer so important to say every morning. What could be more important for a Christian to say every morning, "Lord, please lead me not into temptation, deliver me from temptation, give me the power of the Holy Spirit in my life so that no temptation should overtake me or affect me." He promises to deliver us from all evil, deliver us from all lying, from all evil intent, and from anything that dishonors or disobeys Him. May no evil grip us each day. Let temptation roll off us like water off a duck's back. That is so powerful for living a victorious Christian life.

Then He says, "For thine is the kingdom, and the power and the glory, forever." Essentially, He is ending that prayer saying we can do all of these things because He has opened us up to His kingdom and all of its majesty and glory and power, forever and ever. To everyone who receives Him, He is opening up a portion of that kingdom for today, for tomorrow, for this year, until the Rapture, and throughout eternity. So, exercise your rights. Apply for kingdom privileges, and seek the power of the Holy Spirit to function in your life in every day. Worship in His glory, and as you worship the Lord, ask His glory to permeate your soul from the top of your head to the tips of your toes.

When we go to heaven we'll be permanently, totally in

His glory, majesty, and power. But while we are here on this earth, we need to be sure to ask for wisdom every day in everything we do. As a physician, I ask for wisdom in treating my patients in order to do what is best for them. That doesn't mean that I'm always perfect in doing everything right for them. But God has blessed me in tremendous ways with wisdom in doing things that benefit my patients greatly. For example, I started treating stroke and pre-stroke patients with anti-clotting drugs long before it was popular to do so in the medical community. So, I would encourage you to seek wisdom in your spiritual life and wisdom in everything you do, including the personal and professional areas of your life. Solomon didn't ask for riches, He asked for wisdom. And God was faithful to bless Him with riches and wisdom.

> Yet he has not left himself without testimony: He has shown kindness by giving you rain from heaven and crops in their seasons; he provides you with plenty of food and fills your hearts with joy."
>
> —ACTS 14:17

> If my people, who are called by my name, will humble themselves and pray and seek my face and turn from their wicked ways, then I will hear from heaven, and I will forgive their sin and will heal their land.
>
> —2 CHRONICLES 7:14

10

If You're Not Sure, Just Do It

Pray this prayer with your whole heart, mind, and soul

1. To the God of Abraham, Isaac, and Jacob: I love You with all my heart, mind, and soul.

2. I totally forgive anyone who has ever offended me in any way.

3. Lord, I confess that I'm a sinner. I believe that You sent Jesus to die for my sins and that He was raised from the dead for my redemption.

4. Jesus, forgive me for all my sins, cleanse me from all unrighteousness, make me a new creation, and fill me with Your Holy Spirit.

5. I make You the Lord of my life. I will serve You with my body, mind, and soul. If I stumble, I will repent quickly.

6. I will always forgive when I am offended.

7. May the kingdom of God with all His glory, majesty, power, wisdom, favor, forgiveness, healing, provision, and protection come down from heaven to me today.

8. Greater is the power of the Holy Spirit within me than any stronghold in my life.

9. Then pray the Lord's Prayer each and every day. God bless you as you make this decision.

If you declare with your mouth, "Jesus is Lord," and believe in your heart that God raised him from the dead, you will be saved. For it is with your heart that you believe and are justified, and it is with your mouth that you profess your faith and are saved.

—ROMANS 10:9–10

Afterword

A Note from the Author

I TRUST THAT THIS book will open up a new chapter in your life. I pray that it will turn your life around. Also, I pray for our nation's leaders, from President Obama and the Congress to all the judges including the Supreme Court, and all of our government officials both state and local, to honor His laws. Pray with me that God will give our nation leaders who recognize that our freedom is a blessing from God and that we need to honor His commandments.

But first of all, ask God if there is anything in your life that is displeasing to Him so that you can repent first and get right with Him. As we repent, God will honor us with righteous leaders.

May God's richest blessings be upon you in a mighty way as you choose to serve Him with all your heart, all your mind, and all your soul. May you experience the power of His Holy Spirit, His presence, His glory, and begin to prepare now for His coming again because that glorious day is approaching. Every day, we are one step closer to eternity.

Amen.

About *the* Author

CLARENCE MAST WAS born and raised in the Dover Delaware area of Amish-Mennonite parents. He graduated from the University of Delaware with a BS in Chemistry and worked at Dupont's Central Research Department. He later graduated from Temple University School of Medicine with further studies at Robert Packer Hospital in Sayre, Pennsylvania. He became Board Certified in Family Practice in 1976 and today maintains a part-time general family practice.